STUDY GUIDE

Hath God Said?

R.C. Sproul

LIGONIER MINISTRIES

Renew your Mind.

LIGONIER.ORG | 800-435-4343

421 Ligonier Court, Sanford, FL 32771
E-mail: info@ligonier.org

Printed in China.

1

What Is the Standard of Truth?

INTRODUCTION

Today, not only is the authority of the Bible under attack, but authority as a concept is under attack. In this lecture, Dr. Sproul relates today's crisis over authority to the historic events of the Reformation to show the importance of an objective and absolute standard of truth.

LESSON OBJECTIVES

1. To focus on authority as the formal cause of the Reformation
2. To demonstrate the fundamental similarities between the Reformation's controversy over authority and the problem of cultural relativism

SCRIPTURE READING

And we also thank God constantly for this, that when you received the word of God, which you heard from us, you accepted it not as the word of men but as it really is, the word of God.

—1 Thessalonians 2:13

LECTURE OUTLINE

A. We live in an age characterized by a crisis over authority, a crisis in which Christians cannot escape questions about the trustworthiness of the Bible.

1. For its first 1,800 years, the new covenant church enjoyed a virtually universal confidence in sacred Scripture.
2. In the last two hundred years, the church has experienced a crisis over the authority of Scripture that has spilled over into and become a part of our cultural milieu.

   a. Western culture has experienced a loss of a sense of authority due to scholarly criticism directed toward the Bible.
   b. Around the start of the twentieth century, Abraham Kuyper made the observation that biblical criticism had become biblical vandalism.

B. To understand today's crisis over authority requires an examination of the sixteenth-century Protestant Reformation, which centered on the issue of authority.
   1. The material cause of the Reformation was the debate over justification by faith alone (*sola fide*).
   2. The formal cause of the Reformation was the debate over Scripture as the final authority for faith and life (*sola Scriptura*).
      a. Luther differed with Rome's view on justification to the degree that he was willing to stand against Rome's claims of absolute authority.
      b. Luther refused to recant his views, holding fast to the belief that the Bible is the only source of authority that can bind our consciences.
   3. The Reformation was ultimately a crisis over authority.
      a. Rome maintained that the Bible was established by the church, which places church authority on equal footing with biblical authority.
      b. The Reformers countered that the church received the Bible from God; therefore, the church did not establish the Bible's authority.
   4. The Roman Catholic Church responded to the Reformation by launching the Counter-Reformation, culminating in moral reform and the Council of Trent.
      a. The Council of Trent (1545–63) was Rome's theological response to the Reformation; it opposed *sola fide* and *sola Scriptura*.
      b. In opposition to *sola Scriptura*, the Council of Trent declared that there are two sources of divine authority: Scripture and tradition.
      c. Through this declaration, Rome asserted that the Bible is indeed the infallible Word of God, yet tradition alone infallibly interprets it.
      d. In effect, the Council of Trent made Luther's denial of tradition tantamount to a denial of Scripture itself.

C. The debate over authority during the Protestant Reformation is widely applicable to the crisis over authority in our own day of cultural relativism.
   1. Our day is a day in which the whole concept authority is questioned, resulting in the denial of any standard by which to judge truth.
   2. Authority is defined as "the right to impose obligation," so a denial of authority strikes at the core of our doctrine of Scripture, at God's right to be God.

STUDY QUESTIONS

1. When did the second slogan of the Reformation, *sola Scriptura*, find its pinnacle moment in the life of Martin Luther?
   a. Luther's nailing of the Ninety-Five Theses

b. Luther's public disputation with Johann Eck
c. Luther's public disputation with Thomas Cajetan
d. Luther's defense at the Diet of Worms

2. To which animal was Martin Luther likened in the papal encyclical that announced his excommunication?
   a. Bull
   b. Boar
   c. Swan
   d. Goose

3. Which of the following is an argument the Reformers used against the Roman Catholic Church for the absolute authority of the Bible?
   a. The canon of Scripture was established by the church.
   b. The canon of Scripture was not established by the church.
   c. The church historically used language indicating that Scripture was received.
   d. The councils of the church were all in error before the Reformation.

4. The formal cause of the Reformation was the debate over justification.
   a. True
   b. False

5. What were the conclusions of the Council of Trent regarding the Bible and church tradition?
   a. Scripture is infallible when in agreement with church tradition.
   b. Scripture is fallible yet church tradition corrects it infallibly.
   c. Church tradition is the infallible interpretation of Scripture.
   d. Church tradition is fallible and governed by Scripture.

6. How did Dr. Sproul define authority in this lecture?
   a. The power to enforce laws
   b. The power to establish laws
   c. The right to determine truth
   d. The right to impose obligation

DISCUSSION QUESTIONS

1. In your everyday experience, how do you know what is true? In what ways are your standards for truth objective or subjective? Why?

2. How were the two great concerns of the Reformation—*sola fide* and *sola Scriptura*—related to one another? How does the Reformation teach you the importance of basing your faith and life on the Bible?

3. What do you understand to be the popular concept of authority today? In what ways do you think the Reformation's crisis over authority can be related to modern views of authority in and outside the church?

4. What was fundamentally wrong with the Roman Catholic Church's idea of authority as expressed in the sixteenth century? If core Roman Catholic doctrines were to change relative to justification, would its position on authority still pose a problem for Protestants?

2

Authority & Authorship

INTRODUCTION

For the Bible to be trustworthy, it must be the inerrant Word of God, for this is the very claim it makes about itself. In this lecture, Dr. Sproul connects the concept of authority to authorship so that we see how the root of Scripture's authority is grounded in Scripture's source.

LESSON OBJECTIVES

1. To discuss the necessity of the inerrancy and infallibility of Scripture
2. To examine key passages of Scripture related to authority and authorship

SCRIPTURE READING

No prophecy of Scripture comes from someone's own interpretation. For no prophecy was ever produced by the will of man, but men spoke from God as they were carried along by the Holy Spirit.

—2 Peter 1:20–21

LECTURE OUTLINE

A. Authority, or "the right to impose obligation," is related to ownership and authorship, so the question of biblical authority is inseparably related to biblical authorship.

   1. Historically, the church has confessed the Bible to be the *vox Dei* (voice of God), or more commonly, the *verbum Dei* (the Word of God).
   2. Relative to authority, the source of the Bible is the crux of the issue, so we must address exactly whose words are found in the Bible: man's or God's.
   3. The sixty-six books of the Bible were not physically penned by God.

4. The Bible was written by human beings, but Scripture does point to God as its ultimate author.
    a. In Romans 1:1, Paul identifies himself as the author of the letter, yet he immediately stresses that he is one "set apart for the gospel of God."
    b. The preposition in the phrase "gospel of God" communicates a possessive relationship, announcing the gospel's ultimate source.
5. God is the source of Scripture, which needs to be our upmost consideration when considering the authority of the Bible.
    a. Zechariah was encouraged to believe that Elizabeth would have a child because of the angel Gabriel's divine commission (Luke 1: 19).
    b. Gabriel's pronouncement to Zechariah is analogous to how we are to relate to Scripture as carrying the highest possible authority.

B. Scripture claims for itself the ultimate authority of being the Word of God.
1. The question of Scripture's infallibility might seem to some as a tempest in a teapot, only creating divisions among Christians and unrelated to our faith.
    a. There is no reason that we should require an infallible historical source to have reasonable knowledge about Jesus of Nazareth.
    b. Scripture claims to be the Word of God; therefore, the Bible must be free from error, so the question of infallibility is vitally important.
2. The New Testament places a premium on truthfulness and credibility, so we know that Scripture itself cannot be deceptive or incredible (2 Tim. 3: 13–15).
    a. Paul directly equates deception with evil as he warns Timothy of the danger of false teachers who would infiltrate the life of the church.
    b. Paul encourages Timothy to stand steadfast on the credible ground of the teachings of his youth from the Word of God.
3. Second Timothy 3:16 is the primary text on the infallibility and authority of Scripture.
    a. All Scripture has been "breathed out" by God, which describes how God is the intimate source of all Scripture.
    b. The root of Scripture's authority is grounded in Scripture's source.

STUDY QUESTIONS

1. What is the central issue behind questions about the Bible's authority?
    a. The issue of the Bible's extraordinary claims
    b. The issue of man's sinful ability to suppress the truth
    c. The issue of man's ability to rightly interpret the Bible
    d. The issue of the Bible's ultimate source in man or in God

2. Scripture is the *vox Dei*, the voice of God. What other Latin phrase is often used to convey God's relationship to Scripture?
    a. *Imago Dei*
    b. *Scripta Dei*

  c. *Verbum Dei*
  d. *Veritas Dei*

3. What objection to inerrancy was used by Dr. Sproul's graduate professor?
   a. Inerrancy isn't taught explicitly anywhere in the Bible.
   b. Inerrancy isn't required for accurate historical narrative.
   c. Inerrancy takes away from the way we exercise our faith.
   d. Inerrancy is an American concept foreign to the Bible's context.

4. The Apostles considered only the Old Testament to be the Word of God, because the writing of the New Testament was still in process.
   a. True
   b. False

5. What does Dr. Sproul consider to be an inferior translation of *theopneustos,* despite its being the popular choice of many English translations?
   a. Inspired
   b. Exhaled
   c. Spirit-filled
   d. God-breathed

6. Which Old Testament office relates most to the topic of Scripture's authority as rooted in Scripture's source?
   a. Prophet
   b. Priest
   c. Elder
   d. King

DISCUSSION QUESTIONS

1. Can the Bible be both the Word of God and contain errors or be capable of errors? Why or why not?

2. Besides making claims about itself, how does Scripture support the idea that it must be inerrant and infallible as the Word of God? What are some internal evidences you have found in Scripture that have convinced you of its authority?

3. As Christians, what do we mean by the divine authorship of the Bible? Were people involved in the composition of Scripture? How would you discuss this subject with someone who believes Scripture is merely a man-made product and thus fallible?

4. Do you believe the inerrancy and infallibility of the Bible enhances or takes away from your faith? Why? What does this reveal about the nature of the Christian faith?

3

Inspiration & the Canon of Scripture

INTRODUCTION

The authority of Scripture goes hand in hand with the inspiration and canonicity of the books that make up the Old and New Testaments. In this lecture, Dr. Sproul looks at the process used by the early church to recognize the Word of God so that Christians can be prepared to defend the Bible's authority and authenticity.

LESSON OBJECTIVES

1. To explore the question of the canon and its relationship to authority
2. To describe the process by which the Word of God has been received

SCRIPTURE READING

And count the patience of our Lord as salvation, just as our beloved brother Paul also wrote to you according to the wisdom given him, as he does in all his letters when he speaks in them of these matters. There are some things in them that are hard to understand, which the ignorant and unstable twist to their own destruction, as they do the other Scriptures.

—2 Peter 3:15–16

LECTURE OUTLINE

A. The Bible is a breathtaking collection of sixty-six unique books, and the question of how those books came to be collected is of vital importance for our confidence in the Bible's authority.

1. Questions about which books belong in the Bible are not fundamentally questions about the inspiration of the Bible; this is an important distinction.

   a. Martin Luther believed in the inerrancy of Scripture but at one time questioned whether the epistle of James should be considered Scripture.
   b. Luther called James an "epistle of straw," which has led some to question the doctrine of Scripture that the Reformers held.
   c. Luther's question was not about the inspiration of the Bible but about the canonicity of James—should it properly be included in the Bible?
2. *Canon* is etymologically related to a Greek word that means "a measuring rod, rule, or norm." It is the standard by which other things are judged.
   a. Historically, the collection of books that make up the Bible is called the canon of sacred Scripture.
   b. The question of canonicity is then related to the process by which these books became part of the collection known as the Bible.

B. The canon of the Bible has existed since the first century of the Christian church.
1. Some say the church didn't have a canon for four hundred years; this is a confused view related to the third Council of Carthage's declaration of Scripture's canon in AD 397.
   a. The process by which the canon of Scripture was decided betrays such a claim as a gross oversimplification.
   b. By the second century, in response to Marcion's heretical, Neoplatonic views of God and Scripture, councils acted to affirm the biblical canon.
   c. In the first century, the Apostles quoted one another as authoritative, and the Apostolic fathers likewise quoted the Apostles as authoritative.
2. History tells us that the church did question the canonicity of some books in the New Testament canon, so councils convened to discuss these matters.
   a. Books such as Hebrews, 2 Peter, Jude, and 1, 2, and 3 John were questioned, yet all of these books came to be affirmed as Scripture.
   b. In the process of canonization, only two or three unrecognized books have ever been seriously considered as potentially canonical.

C. The question remains as to how we are to know if we have a purely canonical Bible.
1. The Roman Catholic Church has a facile solution to this problem, proposing that the infallible books of the Bible were collected in an infallible process.
2. Classic Protestantism understands that the infallible books of the Bible were collected in a fallible, yet trustworthy, process.
3. We can have full confidence that the church has recognized the Word of God, which has been faithfully examined on three basic criteria.
   a. A book had to have been written by an Apostle or endorsed by an Apostle.
   b. A book had to have been received by the early church as Scripture.

c. A book had to be free from anything that contradicted the remainder of the New Testament books that were not doubted as canonical.

STUDY QUESTIONS

1. Which council officially declared the canon of Scripture to be closed?
   a. Council of Nicaea in AD 325
   b. Council of Ephesus in AD 431
   c. Third Council of Carthage in AD 397
   d. First Council of Constantinople in AD 381

2. Why is the heretic Marcion important to the discussion about canonicity?
   a. Marcion affirmed an orthodox view of God.
   b. Marcion affirmed only the canonicity of the Old Testament.
   c. Marcion rejected the influence of Gnostic philosophy in the church.
   d. Marcion rejected books of the Bible as early as the second century.

3. What difference exists between a Protestant and a Roman Catholic Bible?
   a. Bibles in the Protestant tradition contain a different New Testament.
   b. Bibles in the Protestant tradition do not contain the catholic epistles.
   c. Bibles in the Roman Catholic tradition contain the Apocrypha.
   d. Bibles in the Roman Catholic tradition do not contain Romans.

4. Compared to the Old Testament, the New Testament is deuterocanonical.
   a. True
   b. False

5. What is the first criterion used by the church to determine which books should be included in the New Testament?
   a. A book would need to have been accepted by the early church.
   b. A book could not contradict the theology of the Old Testament.
   c. A book could not contradict the theology of the New Testament.
   d. A book would need to have been written or endorsed by an Apostle.

6. Of the following New Testament books, which was at one time questioned as to whether it belonged in the canon of sacred Scripture?
   a. Matthew
   b. Romans
   c. Galatians
   d. Hebrews

DISCUSSION QUESTIONS

1. Protestants believe the Bible contains infallible books collected through a fallible process, and Roman Catholics believe the Bible contains infallible books collected through an infallible process. Who is right? Why?

2. Some people are susceptible to the fraudulent claims that certain ancient books, such as the Gnostic gospels, belong in the Bible. How would you help someone see the error of these claims? Does the New Testament give us a sufficient witness to the life of Jesus Christ?

3. How would you answer someone who believes that the New Testament is the only part of the Bible that applies to and is necessary for Christians?

4. Can we have more than a speculative hope that we have the right books in the Bible? How should your view of God influence your answer?

4

Neoorthodoxy & the Canon of Scripture

INTRODUCTION

Neoorthodox theology emerged to combat nineteenth-century liberalism, and yet it failed to espouse a truly orthodox position of Scripture. In this lecture, Dr. Sproul introduces the particular views of Neoorthodox theologians relating to Scripture and the phenomenon of revelation.

LESSON OBJECTIVES

1. To explain the Neoorthodox position of truth as a subjective encounter
2. To explore the orthodox position of Scripture as propositional revelation

SCRIPTURE READING

And beginning with Moses and all the Prophets, he interpreted to them in all the Scriptures the things concerning himself.

—Luke 24:27

LECTURE OUTLINE

A. Neoorthodoxy is a far-reaching theological movement that swept through the world during the first half of the twentieth century, significantly affecting views on Scripture.

1. Karl Barth is the father of Neoorthodox theology and is considered the most famous theologian of the twentieth century.
2. Barth aimed to restore the centrality of the Bible by reversing the skepticism of nineteenth-century liberalism as represented by Friedrich Schleiermacher.

3. Neoorthodoxy, also called crisis theology and dialectical theology, sought a middle ground between liberalism and historic Christianity.
4. Whereas Neoorthodoxy did not outright deny the supernatural dynamics of the Bible, it did not espouse an infallible, verbally inspired, or inerrant Bible.

B. Barth and other theologians, such as Emil Brunner, sought a fresh understanding of the phenomenon of revelation as well as revelation's relationship to truth itself.
1. Neoorthodoxy was a reaction against the affirmation of propositional truth; it taught instead that truth only happens through a subjective encounter.
   a. Neoorthodox theologians were influenced by Søren Kierkegaard, who stressed the passionate, personal involvement of the Christian faith.
   b. Brunner believed that truth is found in encounter, not inherent in the propositional content of revelation itself.
2. Neoorthodoxy therefore views God's revelation in terms of God's action in human history, but the Bible interprets these events for us propositionally.
   a. Revealed events and propositions of the Bible have a given meaning, unlike with abstract art, in which meaning is supplied by the viewer.
   b. The orthodox view of the Bible maintains that God's revelation is inherently truthful and does not depend on our response to it.
3. Neoorthodoxy creates a false dilemma between passion and truth, when in actuality we are called to passionately, subjectively respond to objective truth.

C. Barth made an erroneous distinction between the Bible as the *verbum Dei* and *verba Dei* in that he affirmed the Bible as the Word of God yet not containing the words of God.
1. Barth rejected propositional revelation and so understood the Bible as the Word of God only insofar as it is aided by the Holy Spirit in our experience.
2. The orthodox view maintains that the Bible was verbally inspired by the Holy Spirit and so, from the moment it was written, is always the Word of God.
   a. The Bible is fundamentally propositional, so the historical events of the Bible can only be understood as interpreted by Scripture.
   b. How would we understand the crucifixion of Christ without the meaning given to us by the Apostles?
   c. Even from the biblical witness, we can deduce that experiencing the event alone didn't bring forth the true meaning of the event.
   d. Whereas we can distinguish between events and propositions, we cannot separate them, for Scripture interprets events propositionally.
3. Barth could not grasp the idea that the Bible could be inerrant and penned by fallible people, and thus he failed to perceive the divine superintendence of Scripture.

STUDY QUESTIONS

1. As a theological movement, what was Neoorthodoxy reacting against?

a. Fundamentalism
b. Evangelicalism
c. Liberalism
d. Calvinism

2. What is another name for Neoorthodoxy?
   a. Postliberal theology
   b. Liberation theology
   c. Process theology
   d. Crisis theology

3. Which philosopher was mentioned to have heavily influenced the thought of Neoorthodox theologians such as Karl Barth and Emil Brunner?
   a. Friedrich Nietzsche
   b. Friedrich Schleiermacher
   c. Søren Kierkegaard
   d. Ludwig Wittgenstein

4. Karl Barth believed that the Bible contains the very words of God.
   a. True
   b. False

5. What is true about the tendency and insistence of Neoorthodoxy that we must make a choice between passion and truth?
   a. A choice between passion and truth constrains our actions.
   b. A choice between passion and truth produces a balanced faith.
   c. A choice between passion and truth is required by Scripture.
   d. A choice between passion and truth is a false dilemma.

6. How does Neoorthodoxy mistake the Holy Spirit's role in Scripture?
   a. By denying the Holy Spirit's work in making Scripture the Word of God
   b. By affirming the Holy Spirit's propositional interpretation of Scripture
   c. By denying the Holy Spirit's divine superintendence of Scripture
   d. By affirming the Holy Spirit's personal illumination of Scripture

DISCUSSION QUESTIONS

1. In what sense did Karl Barth regard the Bible as the Word of God? What does the Neoorthodox position regarding truth as an encounter mean?

2. What would the world be like if there was no such thing as propositional knowledge? How does this apply to the Bible? Do you think it would be understandable if it did not contain propositional revelation? Why?

3. How does the crucifixion account of Jesus Christ become an argument for propositional revelation? What examples can you give from this account to prove that truth has a higher standard than pure subjectivism? What other events from the Bible could you use to follow this model of argumentation?

4. How would you respond to someone who says, "The Bible can mean whatever you want it to mean"? How would you explain to them God's character and the work of the Holy Spirit in and through Scripture?

5

Inspiration, Infallibility, & Inerrancy

INTRODUCTION

We serve an infallible and inerrant God. Therefore, His inspired revelation must also be infallible and inerrant. In this lecture, Dr. Sproul defines the doctrines of inspiration, infallibility, and inerrancy while at the same time correcting common misconceptions surrounding them.

LESSON OBJECTIVES

1. To clarify what is meant by the doctrine of the inspiration
2. To distinguish between the doctrines of inerrancy and infallibility

SCRIPTURE READING

"These are the words that you shall speak to the people of Israel." So Moses came and called the elders of the people and set before them all these words that the Lord *had commanded him. All the people answered together and said, "All that the* Lord *has spoken we will do."*

—Exodus 19:6–8

LECTURE OUTLINE

A. Three pivotal concepts inform our study of the authority of Scripture: inspiration, infallibility, and inerrancy—all of which need to be assessed soberly.

1. We must acknowledge the emotional responses, negative connotations, and misconceptions relative to the terms *inspiration*, *infallibility*, and *inerrancy*.
2. The International Council on Biblical Inerrancy began in 1978 to resolve the issues surrounding the meaning and correct use of these terms.

B. The inspiration of Scripture refers to the means or the method by which mere human authors became the instruments or agents of God's divine revelation.

1. The exact details of how the inspiration takes place, which is known as the mode of inspiration, has been left undefined in classical Christian theology.
2. Many misconceptions about the mode of inspiration exist; therefore, we must examine the validity of these misconceptions to rightly understand inspiration.
   a. The authors of Scripture were not mechanically governed by God to pen the words of God; this is known as the mechanical view of inspiration.
   b. The authors of Scripture were not dictated by God as to what was to be written; this is known as the dictation theory of inspiration.
3. The Holy Spirit superintended Scripture in such a way that the vocabulary, style, and experiences of the human authors were freely used for what God intended.

C. The infallibility of Scripture refers to Scripture's incapability of error and as such is a stronger word than inerrancy in our estimation and doctrine of Scripture.

1. The concept of inerrancy evokes a strong visceral reaction, so the concept of infallibility has often been wrongly used to soften statements about Scripture.
2. The preference of the concept of infallibility over inerrancy may be due to a number of factors within the church and culture at large.
   a. Infallibility does not seem to be as emotionally divisive in our culture, which is why inerrancy has been known as a *shibboleth* of orthodoxy.
   b. Infallibility has been favored over inerrancy because of its association with the academic credibility of Jesuits in the Roman Catholic Church.
   c. Infallibility tends to be favored, perhaps most importantly, because the concept of inerrancy is seldom properly defined.

D. The inerrancy of Scripture refers to the fact that Scripture does not contain errors.

1. The doctrine of inerrancy does not mean that the Bible is necessarily free from grammatical errors or that it speaks with absolute scientific precision.
2. The doctrine of inerrancy asserts that there are no errors of truth in the Bible.
   a. The doctrine of inerrancy allows for grammatical idiosyncrasies, round numbers, and literary devices such as hyperbole.
   b. The biblical concept of truth can be defined as communicating a "real state of affairs," a concept of truth to which the Bible itself adheres.
3. The Bible is inspired; therefore, the Bible is infallible; therefore, the Bible is inerrant; therefore, the Bible is altogether trustworthy and true.

STUDY QUESTIONS

1. What theory of divine inspiration is least personal, describing the process of inspiration as if it were an automatic and merely physical procedure?
   a. The dynamic theory of inspiration
   b. The dictation theory of inspiration
   c. The mechanical theory of inspiration
   d. The verbal plenary theory of inspiration

2. From which church council might someone falsely conclude that Roman Catholics believe in the dictation theory of inspiration?
   a. Council of Trent
   b. First Vatican Council
   c. Council of Constance
   d. Second Vatican Council

3. What word has been considered a *shibboleth* of orthodoxy?
   a. Inspiration
   b. Infallibility
   c. Inerrancy
   d. Authority

4. *Infallibility* is a stronger word than *inerrancy* because *inerrancy* simply means that Scripture does not err.
   a. True
   b. False

5. What technical phrase is used to describe the process of inspiration?
   a. The mode of inspiration
   b. The means of inspiration
   c. The method of inspiration
   d. The manner of inspiration

6. Which theologian defined truth—as the term is used in the Bible—as that which communicates a "real state of affairs"?
   a. Paul Tillich
   b. Emil Brunner
   c. Rudolf Bultmann
   d. Friedrich Schleiermacher

DISCUSSION QUESTIONS

1. Why do you think people react emotionally to the term *inerrancy?* If we were to attempt an accommodation for the way people react to it, why would *infallibility* not be the best word to use in its place?

2. Why do you think the church has never precisely defined the way in which the inspiration of Scripture has taken place? Have other attempts to define this process done justice to the doctrine of inspiration? Why or why not?

3. What do you think are the advantages of having a permanent, objective, written revelation of God's acts in history as opposed to other media such as photography or film? In what way does the medium in which God has chosen to reveal Himself give you confidence in the Bible?

4. Imagine someone were to deny the inerrancy of the Bible based on some knowledge of a text-critical or grammatical issue. How would you correct that person's understanding of inerrancy? What examples from Scripture could you use to reinforce your position?

6

Jesus & the Word of God

INTRODUCTION

The issue of the Bible's authority rests on the issue of Christ's authority, such that we cannot believe in one without the other. In this lecture, Dr. Sproul joins the overarching themes of this series to the person of Christ to show why our defense of Scripture as the Word of God is so important.

LESSON OBJECTIVES

1. To correct erroneous views about Scripture relative to the person of Christ
2. To construct an argument for Scripture's reliability as a witness for Christ

SCRIPTURE READING

Scripture cannot be broken.

—John 10:35

LECTURE OUTLINE

A. A question about the Bible's authority is fundamentally a question about Christology.
   1. Our doctrine of Scripture must be governed by what we believe about Jesus.
      a. The fundamental issue is not whether we can trust the Bible but whether we can trust in the authority and truthfulness of Christ.
      b. Scripture is the means by which Christ exercises His authority over us, so our beliefs about Scripture's authority are directly tied to Him.
   2. Jesus believed and understood Scripture to be the Word of God.
      a. The problem of basing our understanding of what Jesus believed on the Bible itself introduces the problem of circular reasoning.

   b. In order to establish the validity of such reasoning, we must proceed linearly and verify the general reliability of the New Testament.

B. The Bible is a reliable historical witness to the life of Jesus Christ.
   1. No ancient book has been submitted to the same rigorous scientific scrutiny that the Bible has undergone, yet the historicity of the Bible has been maintained.
      a. Archaeological evidences that help reconstruct the geography and customs of the ancients support the Bible's historical reliability.
      b. The general consensus even among secular, unreligious scholars is that Luke is the finest historian of the ancient world.
   2. On the basis of the general reliability of the New Testament as a historical document alone, we can become genuinely persuaded that Jesus existed.
      a. The New Testament attests to Jesus' far-reaching acclaim, that He was known to be extraordinary and was recognized as a prophet.
      b. The fact that Jesus was attested to be a prophet is reason alone for us to seriously consider what He taught concerning Scripture.

C. Jesus of Nazareth embraced the full authority of Scripture as the inspired, infallible, and inerrant Word of God in both His humanity and His deity.
   1. There is no serious debate about what Jesus believed about Scripture.
      a. Critics recognize that the most historically validated segment of the New Testament demonstrates Jesus' view of the Bible's authority.
      b. Jesus taught the prevalent view of Scripture held among the Jews, namely, that it is the Word of God (Matt. 4:4; 5:18; John 17:17).
   2. Karl Barth and other modernist theologians hold that Jesus was in error regarding His estimation of Scripture, appealing to His human nature.
      a. In His humanity, Jesus' knowledge was limited (Mark 13:32).
      b. The claim is thus made that Jesus could have been mistaken in His open-armed acceptance of the prevailing Jewish view of Scripture.
   3. To argue against such a position, we may acknowledge that Jesus did not have to be omniscient in order to save us, but He did have to be sinless.
      a. Scripture outlines rigorous and somber standards for those who would teach, that such would come under greater judgment (James 3:1).
      b. Jesus claimed to teach with the authority of the Father—He did not lie; otherwise, by the Bible's own standards, He could not have saved us.

STUDY QUESTIONS

1. What logical dilemma relates to Jesus' beliefs about Scripture?
   a. The fallacy of false dilemma
   b. The fallacy of false authority
   c. The fallacy of circular reasoning
   d. The fallacy of circular consequence

2. Which gospel writer is considered to be the finest ancient historian?
    a. Matthew
    b. Mark
    c. Luke
    d. John

3. How do some theologians rationalize their belief that Jesus erred in His view of Scripture?
    a. By claiming that people misrepresent His view of Scripture
    b. By rejecting the general reliability of the New Testament
    c. By separating His teaching authority from moral standards
    d. By appealing to His human nature and natural limitations

4. Jesus had to be omniscient to be a substitutionary sacrifice for our sins.
    a. True
    b. False

5. Considering the historic reliability of the Bible, even if Jesus were only considered a prophet, why is this important for His view of Scripture?
    a. A prophet's words were spoken with an inherent infallibility.
    b. A prophet's words were subject to the standard of God's law.
    c. A prophet's words were sometimes infallible yet always reliable.
    d. A prophet's words were said to divine the outcome of the future.

6. At what level must the inerrancy of the Bible be steadfastly maintained?
    a. At the level of the original manuscripts
    b. At the level of the copied manuscripts
    c. At the level of the English translations
    d. At the level of the original languages

DISCUSSION QUESTIONS

1. Many people have deep philosophical difficulty with an inerrant Bible in an error-filled world. What is in jeopardy if we were never to offer a defense of the Bible against such difficulties?

2. How do we avoid the accusation of circular reasoning when appealing to Christ's understanding of Scripture? Do you think circular reasoning is always an invalid form of reasoning? Why or why not?

3. Why is it impossible to submit to Christ's lordship without believing in the inspiration, infallibility, and inerrancy of the Bible? In light of this, why is the Bible significant for Christian growth?

4. What reasons have you heard people use to justify their rejection of the Bible's authority or inerrancy? Do you think their main contention is with the Bible itself or something else?

STUDY GUIDE ANSWER KEY

Lesson 1

1. D
2. B
3. C
4. B
5. C
6. D

Lesson 2

1. D
2. C
3. C
4. B
5. A
6. A

Lesson 3

1. C
2. D
3. C
4. B
5. D
6. D

Lesson 4

1. C
2. D
3. C
4. B
5. D
6. C

Lesson 5

1. C
2. A
3. C
4. A
5. A
6. C

Lesson 6

1. C
2. C
3. D
4. B
5. B
6. A

LESSON 1:

1. It was during his defense at the Diet of Worms that *sola scriptura* had reached its pinnacle moment in the life of Martin Luther and in the life of the Reformation. At the Diet of Worms, Luther firmly stood his ground saying, "My conscience is held captive by the Word of God. I cannot and I will not recant anything for to go against conscience is neither right nor safe. God help me. Amen."

2. The first words of the papal bull of Luther's excommunication were "Rise up, O Lord," followed by a comparison of Luther to a wild boar destroying a vineyard, which in the eyes of Rome, of course meant the church. Interestingly, Jan Hus, whose name means "goose," before being burned at the stake said, "Today you burn a goose, but in one hundred years a swan will arise which you will prove unable to boil or roast." One cannot help but think of Luther in these words.

3. The Reformers argued against the Roman Catholic Church's claim that because the canon of Scripture was established by the church then the church had equal authority with Scripture. They did so by showing how the church councils that played a part in determining the canon acknowledged that Scripture was ultimately received by the church from God.

4. The debate over justification was the material cause of the Reformation, and the debate over authority was the formal cause of the Reformation. The debate over justification caused an even deeper debate over the authority of Scripture, which clearly teaches the Reformation distinctive that justification is by faith alone.

5. The Council of Trent was the Roman Catholic Church's formal response to the Reformation, and concerning the matter of authority, it declared that there are two sources of divine authority, both Scripture and tradition. Therefore, church tradition was deemed to have the authority to infallibly interpret the Bible.

6. Dr. Sproul defined authority as "the right to impose obligation." This definition captures the true sense of authority, for it stresses one's right to control and not merely one's power to control. Some answer choices emphasized power but not necessarily right. God, as God, has the supreme right to impose obligation, and His authority is always governed by His righteous character; it is not tyrannical.

LESSON 2:

1. The crux of the dispute relative to the authority of the Bible comes down to the issue of the Bible's source, whether it's ultimately a product of God or man. We know that the Bible is the Word of God, and because God is its ultimate author, we can trust that it is authoritative, inerrant, and infallible.

2. Dr. Sproul used two Latin phrases to capture the church's historical confession about Scripture, *vox Dei* and *verbum Dei*. The first phrase, *vox Dei*, means "the voice of God." The second phrase, *verbum Dei*, means "the Word of God." Both phrases communicate Scripture's ultimate source and authority.

3. Whereas it is possible to have accurate historical narratives without inerrancy, the main objection of Dr. Sproul's graduate professor was that inerrancy takes away from our exercise of faith. He believed that the quest for certainty that is central to the debates about inerrancy deprives us of simply believing God, yet we must acknowledge what Scripture reveals about itself, that God is speaking to us through it; therefore, it cannot err.

4. The Apostles certainly considered the Old Testament to be the Word of God, but they also considered their own writings to be the inspired Word of God. Apostles were given authority by none other than Christ, and so when they referenced the letters of other Apostles, they gave them the full weight of that authority (2 Peter 3:15–16).

5. Despite being a popular choice among many English translations in 2 Timothy 3:16, Dr. Sproul noted "inspired" was an inferior translation of *theopneustos*, which can be more literally translated as "God-breathed" or "breathed out by God." "Inspired" denotes breathing into something, whereas *theopneustos* denotes breathing out, pointing to the authoritative source of Scripture.

6. The Old Testament office which most closely relates to Scripture's authority as rooted in Scripture's source is the prophetical office. Dr. Sproul demonstrated this by highlighting how Old Testament prophets would say, "Thus says the Lord," and not, "Thus says Jeremiah" or "Thus says Isaiah."

LESSON 3:

1. It was in 397 AD during the third Council of Carthage that the canon of Scripture was officially declared to be closed. While this council verges on the fifth century, the church had an understanding of sacred Scripture from the first century, and it would be a gross misconception to think that

the church did not have a Bible for 500 years, a common and ignorant miscalculation discredited by Dr. Sproul.

2. Marcion's heretical views were infused with a gnostic philosophy that resulted in his rejection of various books of the Bible as early as the second century. This is important to the question of canonicity because it proves that the church viewed certain books to be canonical as early as the second century, which is essential for Marcion to reject them in the first place.

3. Bibles in the Protestant and the Roman Catholic tradition contain considerable agreement in that all of the books considered canonical by Protestants are also considered canonical by Roman Catholics. The key exception to this is that the seven books known as the Apocrypha are also included by Roman Catholics. The catholic epistles are the New Testament letters universal in nature, not written to specific churches, such as James and 1 and 2 Peter among others.

4. Both the Old Testament and the New Testament are canonical, standing equally as the one true Word of God. The term deuterocanonical denotes a secondary level of authority, and in this lecture, was used to describe an appropriate view of the Apocrypha.

5. The first criterion used to decide which books belonged in the New Testament as the inspired Word of God was the book's apostolic authority. In this, a book to be even considered would have to be written or endorsed by an apostle, and then it would be examined on the basis of its theological consistency and credibility in the early church.

6. Hebrews was at one time questioned in church history as to whether or not it was canonical. The apostolicity of Matthew, Romans, and Galatians was undeniable, but Hebrews contained various passages that can be difficult to interpret related to the nature of salvation (Heb. 6:4–6). Nevertheless, the church would go on to receive the Epistle to the Hebrews for what it is—the Word of God.

LESSON 4:

1. Neoorthodoxy reacted against the nineteenth-century liberalism characterized by the theology of such men as Friedrich Schleiermacher. Neoorthodoxy thus sought to restore confidence in the Bible after the rank skepticism of liberalism, yet it attempted to do so without affirming essential orthodox positions on Scripture, such as Scripture's inerrancy and inspiration.

2. Neoorthodoxy arose out of the disillusionment of the First World War, so it is no surprise that it is known as "crisis theology." This is primarily due to the emphasis of neoorthodoxy on the necessity of faith and revelation to overcome the crises of the human condition, both individually and institutionally.

3. The philosopher who heavily influenced neoorthodox theology, especially in the thought of Emil Brunner, was the nineteenth-century Danish philosopher Soren Kierkegaard. Kierkegaard influenced rejection of propositional revelation in neoorthodox theology because of his concern for a subjective, passionate Christian faith.

4. Barth made a distinction between Scripture as the *verba Dei* and Scripture as the *verbum Dei*, rejecting entirely that Scripture could be the *verba Dei*, which means "the words of God." It is difficult to understand how Barth could call Scripture "the Word of God" and yet believe that Scripture did not contain "words of God," but this is due to his rejection of propositional revelation and emphasis on the work of the Holy Spirit to transform the words of the Bible into the Word of God.

5. The neoorthodox interpretation of the phenomena of revelation and the nature of truth itself creates a false dilemma in which we are told to choose between truth or passion. In actuality, as Christians, we are called to be passionate for truth, exercising a true subjective faith, but never at the expense of objective truth.

6. Neoorthodoxy may appear to have a strong theology of the Holy Spirit because it makes much of the Holy Spirit's work in revelation, but it fails to do justice to the Holy Spirit's power. The Holy Spirit powerfully superintended the writing of Holy Scripture, such that He conquered man's weakness to deliver to us the inspired, infallible, and inerrant Word of God.

LESSON 5:

1. The theory of divine inspiration which is least personal is the mechanical theory of inspiration. The reason why it is the least personal theory of inspiration is that the human authors of Scripture are reduced to automatons. The dictation theory can also be said to be impersonal, but this theory at least gives the authors of Scripture some level of agency.

2. The Latin word *dictante* was used with reference to Scripture during the Council of Trent, and from the use of this word some may erroneously derive the notion that Roman Catholics believe in the dictation theory of

inspiration. The dictation theory of inspiration is not intended to be conveyed by *dictante*, only that there is some comparison of the authors of Scripture to amanuenses.

3. Inerrancy has often been considered the *shibboleth* of orthodoxy. *Shibboleth* is a term taken from Judges 12, where the Ephraimites could not pronounce the word *shibboleth*, revealing their true identity as Ephraimites. The term has come to be used to delineate the distinctive qualities of those who would be considered inside from those who would be considered outside.

4. "Infallibility" is a stronger word than "inerrancy," because even a human being can write something that is inerrant, something that is without error. Such inerrancy, on a human level, is merely temporary, because we are radically prone to error. On the other hand, infallibility is the inability to err altogether.

5. Dr. Sproul used the technical term "mode" to describe the process of inspiration. There are many misconceptions about the mode of inspiration, as reviewed in this lesson, such the mechanical theory and the dictation theory of inspiration. These theories fall short in describing the exact way God has sovereignly used unique individuals to pen His very own Word in Scripture.

6. Rudolf Bultmann defined truth as communicating a "real state of affairs" in *The Theological Dictionary of the New Testament*, which is significant because of Bultmann's renown as a liberal theologian. By the Bible's own standard of truthfulness, it must be the inspired, infallible, and inerrant Word of God.

LESSON 6:

1. A vicious circle exists when discussing what Jesus believed about Scripture and may allow the accusation of circular reasoning. This is because we cannot know what Jesus believed without going to the only infallible source of what Jesus believed, namely, the Bible.

2. The Bible has undergone significant scientific scrutiny to determine its historical reliability. From such research, even secular scholars have concluded that Luke is the finest historian of the ancient world regarding his historical accuracy as supported by archeology and other historical documents.

3. Most significantly, theologians who deny the inerrancy of the Bible appeal to the human nature of Christ to rationalize how it is that Jesus could err regarding the true nature of Scripture. A good counterargument to this flawed opinion would be to demonstrate how such theologians divorce what Jesus taught about Scripture from the Bible's high moral standards for a teacher.

4. Jesus Christ is truly God and truly man, two natures in one person. Touching His human nature, Jesus was not omniscient. Omniscience was not an attribute that was necessary for Jesus to fully identify with us as our Mediator before God. On the other hand, sinless perfection was a necessary attribute for Him to be qualified to take upon our sin as a substitutionary sacrifice.

5. Even if the Bible's inerrancy were not granted at the outset, it should be deemed historically reliable. Thus, it would be fair to acknowledge that Jesus was at least considered to be a prophet. This is significant within the context of the nation of Israel, because a prophet was subject to the law of God, which demanded nothing short of death as a punishment for falsehood.

6. The Bible is the inerrant Word of God, and orthodoxy maintains that the Bible is guaranteed to be inerrant at the level of the original manuscripts. Languages, copyists, and translators are all susceptible to error. Despite this fact, there is overwhelming agreement in the copies of theses original manuscripts that evidence the way God has preserved His Word throughout the ages.